Kelly Holmes

by

Andy Croft

Illustrated by Colin Howard

First published in 2007 in Great Britain by
Barrington Stoke Ltd
18 Walker St, Edinburgh, EH3 7LP

www.barringtonstoke.co.uk

ISBN: 978-1-84299-511-2

Printed in Great Britain by Bell & Bain Ltd

A Note from the Author

I used to run a lot. Half marathons, mostly.
I was never very fast. But I always enjoyed it.
These days my knees are dodgy, so I've stopped
running on roads. But I miss it.

What do I miss? The pain, the sweat and the
misery. Getting hurt and being knackered. I miss
running in bad weather, and being chased by big
dogs. Running isn't always a lot of fun. But it's
all worth it when you cross the finishing line.

Kelly Holmes knows all about the pain and the
misery of running. But she also knows a bit about
winning. And she knows that you won't win
anything if you don't try.

For all the kids at The Meadows School
in Spennymoor, County Durham

Contents

Chapter 1

Pure Gold

The story of Kelly Holmes is like a fairy-tale. And like the best fairy-tales, it has a happy ending.

It's full of ups and downs. But if Kelly Holmes is knocked down, she always bounces back. She wants to be the best. She is the best.

Kelly Holmes is a winner. A gold-medal winner. Kelly Holmes is pure gold.

Chapter 2

On Your Marks

Kelly Holmes was born on 19 April 1970, in Pembury, Kent. Her dad comes from Jamaica. Her mum is English. They split up before her first birthday. Kelly and her mum, Pam, moved to London. They didn't have much money. They lived in a tiny flat in New Cross. Pam had to go out to work, so she couldn't look after the baby. She put Kelly in a Children's Home until she was four. She even thought about having Kelly adopted.

When Kelly was seven, her mum married a house painter called Mick. Kelly calls him her "real dad". They moved back to Kent. Soon Kelly had two little brothers called Stuart and Kevin.

Kelly went to Hildenborough Primary School. She was a bit of a tomboy, with big afro hair. She was always getting into fights.

She joined the Brownies. At the school sports day she won the egg and spoon race and the sack race!

Next, Kelly went to Hugh Christie Secondary School in Tonbridge. She used to ride her bike to school every day. Kelly was not very good at school work, but she always tried hard.

PE was her best subject. She was good at gym and judo. She played netball and hockey for the school. In the summer, Kelly ran on

the track. In the winter, she ran cross-country.

When she was 12, she joined Tonbridge Athletics Club. There she met a coach called Dave Arnold. He knew that Kelly was special. They started training together. When she was 13, Kelly was the Kent Schools 1500 metres champion. She won the English Schools Junior 1500 metres the following year, and then again in 1987.

In her last year at school she was picked to run for Britain in the European Youth

Olympics in Holland. She ran in the 800 metres. Of course she won.

Kelly's idols were Olympic medal-winners Sebastian Coe and Tessa Sanderson. She used to dream of running in the Olympics. Perhaps one day she would win an Olympic medal ...

But first she had to earn a living.

Chapter 3

In the Army

Kelly left school at 16. She wanted to join the Army, but she was too young. So she worked in a newsagent's shop and then in a hospital.

A year later she joined the Army. She trained to be a lorry driver. Private Holmes loved the army. She liked the hard work and the rules. And she liked driving big, heavy lorries. But she was not very good at map-reading. She kept getting lost!

Soon Kelly was running in Army sports competitions. She was Army champion at the 200 metres, the 400 metres (three times), the 800 metres (twice) and the 1500 metres. She was also the Army judo champion. Once, Kelly raced against the fastest men in the Army – and she beat them all!

Kelly trained as an Army Gym Instructor. It was hard. But she loved it, most of all the assault courses. She went rock-climbing and skiing. She learned how to coach and referee volleyball, judo, badminton and tennis. She liked being in the gym all day. The only sport she didn't like was canoeing. Kelly was afraid of the water!

She ran against the best athletes in the RAF, the Navy and the Army. But Kelly was the best. She won the 200 metres, the 400 metres (twice), the 800 metres, the 1500 metres (twice) and the 3000 metres.

One day Kelly was watching the Olympics on TV. She suddenly saw someone she knew among the British runners. Kelly had raced against her when they were younger. And Kelly had almost always won. If that girl was good enough to run in the Olympics, then so could Kelly. She rang up her old coach Dave Arnold. Would he help her train again? Of course he would.

Kelly joined the Army Youth Team in London. This meant she was working with teenagers who wanted to join the Army. She

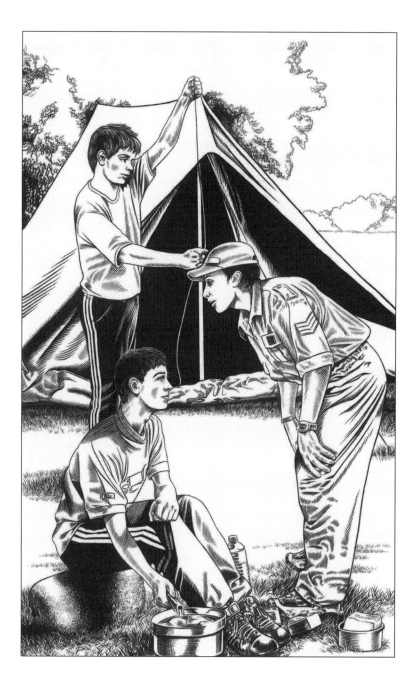

took them camping. This way she could train more often with Dave Arnold.

But it was hard trying to train while she was still in the Army. Kelly loved the Army life. By now she was Sergeant Kelly. But she needed to spend more time training. So in 1997, Kelly left the Army.

Chapter 4

Highs

At first, everything went well for Kelly.

At the 1993 World Championships in Germany, she broke the English record for 800 metres.

The next year she won the silver medal in the 1500 metres in the European Championships in Finland. Her first medal! At the 1994 Commonwealth Games in Canada she won the gold medal in the 1500 metres. Her first gold medal!

The following year she came second in the 1500 metres and third in the 800 metres in the World Championships in Sweden.

In 1996 she won the AAA (Amateur Athletics Association) 800 metres *and* the

1500 metres. No one had ever done this before!

In 1997 she broke the British and Commonwealth records for the 800 metres, 1000 metres and 1500 metres. At the 1998 Commonwealth Games Kelly won the silver medal for the 1500 metres. And at the 2002 Commonwealth Games in Manchester, Kelly won the gold medal for the 1500 metres.

Next stop, the Olympics ...

Chapter 5

Lows

In 1996 she was picked to run for Britain in the Atlanta Olympics. But it all went wrong. Kelly hurt her left leg before the Games. The doctors gave her lots of pain-killers, but it still hurt. In spite of the pain, she reached the 800 metre final. But she was beaten into fourth place by 0.1 of a second.

The pain in Kelly's leg was getting worse. But she still battled through to the 1500 metre final. In the final, Kelly was leading with one lap left, but she couldn't keep going. Her leg hurt too much. In the end Kelly came last. She was very upset. She came home on crutches.

Being a top athlete can be lonely, most of all when things go wrong. And lots of things went wrong for Kelly.

At the World Championships in Greece, Kelly hurt her leg. She dropped out in her

first race. When she came home she needed an operation on her ankle. After that she was out of action for a year.

Just before the Sydney Olympics in 2000, Kelly hurt her back in a cross-country race.

She could not feel her right leg. But she carried on training. Every day she did hours on the step-machine, cycling machines or in the pool. And then she did weights. But it wasn't enough. But she did come third in the 800 metre final and seventh in the 1500 metres.

Kelly was ill just before the 2001 World Championships in Canada. It made her feel very tired. She did reach the 800 metre final, and she came sixth.

Two years later, Kelly had a new problem with her left knee. It hurt when she tried to run. She thought she would never get better. She was unhappy, angry and depressed. She started hurting herself with a pair of scissors to try and make the upset go away but now she knows that it was not a good idea.

At the 2004 World Indoor Championships Kelly tripped over and hurt herself.

Would she ever win an Olympic medal? Some people said she tried too hard. Some people said she wasn't good enough. Some people said she was too old.

But Kelly never gave up. When things were looking bad, she remembered a little poem she once read:

Stick to the fight when you are

hardest hit,

It's when things seem worst that you

must never quit.

And Kelly never quit.

Chapter 6

Double Gold

In 2004 the Olympic Games were held in Athens. Of course, Kelly was chosen again to run for Britain. It was her last chance to win an Olympic medal. Could she do it this time? Or was she too old?

Some people thought she should run in the 800 metres. Some people said she should run in the 1500 metres. Kelly decided to run in both. No one had ever tried to run in both races at three Olympics before. Could she do it? Would she be unlucky again?

So that she did not get injured again, Kelly had to stand in a bucket of ice every day to make her legs stronger. Two weeks before the Games, Kelly had a nasty insect bite.

Kelly easily won the 800 metres heat. She won the semi-final. Kelly was in the final. But could she win it?

The night before the final she tried to relax. She watched *Finding Nemo*. And she kept playing her favourite Alicia Keyes song, 'If I Ain't Got You'.

The next day Kelly was racing against the very best – three time world champion Maria Mutola and the current European champion Jolanda Ceplak. Kelly started at the back. At

the bell she tried to move forward, but someone blocked her. She tried again on the bend, but she was blocked again. On the last bend she ran out wide until she was level with Maria Mutola. With only 10 metres to go Kelly pulled in front. Almost there. 10 metres, 9, 8, 7, 6, 5, 4, 3, 2 – Kelly crossed the finishing line just ahead of Ceplak and Mutola. Yes! Olympic gold!

But Kelly couldn't have a party yet. The next day she had to run in the 1500 metres heat. She was very tired. But she came second. She came second again in the semi-final. It meant that she was in another Olympic final. This time she was running against the world champion from Russia. Could Kelly really do it again?

Again she started slowly, right at the back. But then she began to overtake the other runners. With 90 metres left she took the lead. With 50 metres left she kicked for home. The crowd went wild. Yes! Yes! Another gold medal for Kelly!

It was a new British record of 3 minutes, 57.90 seconds. Kelly was the first British

woman ever to be a double Olympic champion. No British athlete had won two gold medals in the same Olympics for over 80 years. Amazing! Pure gold!

After 20 years of dreaming, Kelly Holmes was an Olympic champion at last.

Chapter 7

I Am What I Am

When Kelly arrived back in Britain she went to see her mum. 40,000 people turned out to welcome her on the streets of Tonbridge.

Kelly Holmes is now very famous. She has bought a house in South Africa. She likes wearing diamonds and designer dresses.

She was voted BBC Sports Personality of the Year, International Athlete of the Year, European Female Athlete of the Year and World Female Athlete in 2005. Kelly has been on *Parkinson* with Tom Cruise, and on the *Ant and Dec Show* with Robbie Williams. She has been on *Desert Island Discs*, in an *Eastenders* Christmas Special, and in *Dancing On Ice*. She has met Pelé. She has presented the MOBO awards and launched an ocean-liner. The Queen gave her an MBE in 1998, and a DBE in 2005 (this means she is now 'Dame' Kelly Holmes!)

In 2005, Kelly decided it was time to retire from running. But today she is busier than ever. She was part of the team that helped London bid for the 2012 Olympics. She spends a lot of time raising money for breast cancer, self-harm and anti-bullying charities. She works for Sports Relief and the Dreams Come True charity.

As National School Sports Champion,
Kelly travels round the UK visiting schools.
Her job is to inspire young people, most of all
girls, to enjoy sport.

She has two Chinese tattoos on her
shoulder. One says, "The Will to Win". The
other says, "Strength, Power and Success".
Together they mean "exceptional victory".

She has just started a training
programme in Great Britain and South Africa
for girls who want to run like Kelly. It is

called "On Camp with Kelly". She wants to teach the girls to be the best. Just like Kelly. She says that "to succeed in any walk of life you must have passion, desire and the will win."

Just like Kelly Holmes.

Chapter 8

Ten Things You May Not Know About Kelly

Kelly may be famous, but she is also a very private person. She doesn't like talking about herself. But here are a few things that not many people know about Kelly:

1. She wears glasses.

2. She suffers from asthma.

3. She hates smoking.

4. She doesn't like cold weather.

5. She is a judo blue-belt.

6. Her favourite food is Chinese.

7. Her favourite music is R'n'B

   and Tina Turner.

8. She has two dogs, called Whitney and

   Barney.

9. She loves chocolate.

10. And she is still afraid of water!

Chapter 9

Kelly's Medals

Gold

2004 Olympic Games, 1500 metres

2004 Olympic Games, 800 metres

2002 Commonwealth Games, 1500 metres

1994 Commonwealth Games, 1500 metres

Silver

2003 World Championships, 800 metres

2003 World Indoor Championships,

1500 metres

2001 Goodwill Games, 800 metres

1998 Commonwealth Games, 1500 metres

1995 World Championships, 1500 metres

1994 European Championships, 1500 metres

Bronze

2002 European Championships, 800 metres

2000 Olympic Games, 800 metres

1995 World Championships, 800 metres

AAA 800 metres champion

2004, 2001, 2000, 1999, 1996, 1995, 1993

AAA 1500 metres champion

2002, 1996, 1994

UK 800 metres champion

1997, 1993

English Schools 1500 metres champion

1987, 1983

Barrington Stoke would like to thank all its readers for commenting on the manuscript before publication and in particular:

Alison McMahan

Rose Magill

Daniella Mann

Become a Consultant!

Would you like to give us feedback on our titles before they are published? Contact us at the email address below – we'd love to hear from you!

info@barringtonstoke.co.uk
www.barringtonstoke.co.uk

Great reads – no problem!

Barrington Stoke books are:

Great stories – from thrillers to comedy to horror, and all by the best writers around!

No hassle – fast reads with no boring bits, and a story that doesn't let go of you till the last page.

Short – the perfect size for a fast, fun read.

We use our own font and paper to make it easier to read our books. And we ask teenagers like you, who want a no-hassle read, to check every book before it's published.

That way, we know for sure that every Barrington Stoke book is a great read for everyone.

Check out www.barringtonstoke.co.uk for more info about Barrington Stoke and our books!

If you loved this book

why don't you read ...

Kiss of Death

by Charles Butler

Kate wants Nick
Nothing will stop her.
Not even *death* ...

gr8reads

You can order *Kiss of Death* directly from our website at
www.barringtonstoke.co.uk

If you loved this book

why don't you read ...

Gremlin

by Chris Powling

The pilot is sick
The plane will crash
Can Glenn save it?

gr8reads

If you loved this book
why don't you read ...

Death Leap
by Simon Chapman

Jake saw a murder
The killers saw Jake
Now the killers are after him ...

gr8reads

You can order *Death Leap* directly from our website at
www.barringtonstoke.co.uk

If you loved this book

why don't you read ...

Thing
by Chris Powling

Black button eyes
Zig-zag mouth
Stiff body
Thing

Once it was Robbie's best friend.

Now it's become his enemy ...

gr8reads

You can order *Thing* directly from our website at
www.barringtonstoke.co.uk